Nautical Log Book

NAUTICAL LOG

Date

From: _____   Towards: _____

Time	Course	Log	Comments	Watch Leader
0100				
0200				
0300				
0400				
0500				
0600				
0700				
0800				
0900				
1000				
1100				
1200				
1300				
1400				
1500				
1600				
1700				
1800				
1900				
2000				
2100				
2200				
2300				
2400				

Watches Set

Time	Leader	Crew	Time	Leader	Crew

NAUTICAL LOG

Constant Port: _____   1st High Water: _____   1st Low Water: _____

_____   2nd High Water: _____   2nd Low Water: _____

Local Port: _____   1st High Water: _____   1st Low Water: _____

_____   2nd High Water: _____   2nd Low Water: _____

M Compass			Position		Boat		Wind		Barometer	Sea State		Sky Cond
Varia	Devia	True	Latitude	Longitude	Speed	RPM	Speed	Dir		Dir	Ft	

_____

Signed

NAUTICAL LOG

Date

From: _____   Towards: _____

Time	Course	Log	Comments	Watch Leader
0100				
0200				
0300				
0400				
0500				
0600				
0700				
0800				
0900				
1000				
1100				
1200				
1300				
1400				
1500				
1600				
1700				
1800				
1900				
2000				
2100				
2200				
2300				
2400				

Watches Set

Time	Leader	Crew	Time	Leader	Crew

NAUTICAL LOG

Constant Port: _____   1st High Water: _____   1st Low Water: _____

_____   2nd High Water: _____   2nd Low Water: _____

Local Port: _____   1st High Water: _____   1st Low Water: _____

_____   2nd High Water: _____   2nd Low Water: _____

M Compass			Position		Boat		Wind		Barometer	Sea State		Sky Cond
Varia	Devia	True	Latitude	Longitude	Speed	RPM	Speed	Dir		Dir	Ft	

_____

Signed

NAUTICAL LOG

Date

From: _____   Towards: _____

Time	Course	Log	Comments	Watch Leader
0100				
0200				
0300				
0400				
0500				
0600				
0700				
0800				
0900				
1000				
1100				
1200				
1300				
1400				
1500				
1600				
1700				
1800				
1900				
2000				
2100				
2200				
2300				
2400				

Watches Set

Time	Leader	Crew	Time	Leader	Crew

NAUTICAL LOG

Constant Port: _____ 1ˢᵗ High Water: _____ 1ˢᵗ Low Water: _____

_____ 2ⁿᵈ High Water: _____ 2ⁿᵈ Low Water: _____

Local Port: _____ 1ˢᵗ High Water: _____ 1ˢᵗ Low Water: _____

_____ 2ⁿᵈ High Water: _____ 2ⁿᵈ Low Water: _____

M Compass			Position		Boat		Wind		Barometer	Sea State		Sky Cond
Varia	Devia	True	Latitude	Longitude	Speed	RPM	Speed	Dir		Dir	Ft	

_____

Signed

NAUTICAL LOG

Date

From: _____ Towards: _____

Time	Course	Log	Comments	Watch Leader
0100				
0200				
0300				
0400				
0500				
0600				
0700				
0800				
0900				
1000				
1100				
1200				
1300				
1400				
1500				
1600				
1700				
1800				
1900				
2000				
2100				
2200				
2300				
2400				

Watches Set

Time	Leader	Crew	Time	Leader	Crew

NAUTICAL LOG

Constant Port: _____ 1st High Water: _____ 1st Low Water: _____

_____ 2nd High Water: _____ 2nd Low Water: _____

Local Port: _____ 1st High Water: _____ 1st Low Water: _____

_____ 2nd High Water: _____ 2nd Low Water: _____

M Compass			Position		Boat		Wind		Barometer	Sea State		Sky Cond
Varia	Devia	True	Latitude	Longitude	Speed	RPM	Speed	Dir		Dir	Ft	

_____
Signed

NAUTICAL LOG

Date

From: _____   Towards: _____

Time	Course	Log	Comments	Watch Leader
0100				
0200				
0300				
0400				
0500				
0600				
0700				
0800				
0900				
1000				
1100				
1200				
1300				
1400				
1500				
1600				
1700				
1800				
1900				
2000				
2100				
2200				
2300				
2400				

Watches Set

Time	Leader	Crew	Time	Leader	Crew

NAUTICAL LOG

Constant Port: _____   1st High Water: _____   1st Low Water: _____

_____   2nd High Water: _____   2nd Low Water: _____

Local Port: _____   1st High Water: _____   1st Low Water: _____

_____   2nd High Water: _____   2nd Low Water: _____

M Compass			Position		Boat		Wind		Barometer	Sea State		Sky Cond
Varia	Devia	True	Latitude	Longitude	Speed	RPM	Speed	Dir		Dir	Ft	

_____
Signed

NAUTICAL LOG

Date

From: _____   Towards: _____

Time	Course	Log	Comments	Watch Leader
0100				
0200				
0300				
0400				
0500				
0600				
0700				
0800				
0900				
1000				
1100				
1200				
1300				
1400				
1500				
1600				
1700				
1800				
1900				
2000				
2100				
2200				
2300				
2400				

Watches Set

Time	Leader	Crew	Time	Leader	Crew

NAUTICAL LOG

Constant Port: _____   1st High Water: _____   1st Low Water: _____

_____   2nd High Water: _____   2nd Low Water: _____

Local Port: _____   1st High Water: _____   1st Low Water: _____

_____   2nd High Water: _____   2nd Low Water: _____

M Compass			Position		Boat		Wind		Barometer	Sea State		Sky Cond
Varia	Devia	True	Latitude	Longitude	Speed	RPM	Speed	Dir		Dir	Ft	

_____

Signed

NAUTICAL LOG

Date

From: _____   Towards: _____

Time	Course	Log	Comments	Watch Leader
0100				
0200				
0300				
0400				
0500				
0600				
0700				
0800				
0900				
1000				
1100				
1200				
1300				
1400				
1500				
1600				
1700				
1800				
1900				
2000				
2100				
2200				
2300				
2400				

Watches Set

Time	Leader	Crew	Time	Leader	Crew

NAUTICAL LOG

Constant Port: _____   1st High Water: _____   1st Low Water: _____

_____   2nd High Water: _____   2nd Low Water: _____

Local Port: _____   1st High Water: _____   1st Low Water: _____

_____   2nd High Water: _____   2nd Low Water: _____

M Compass			Position		Boat		Wind		Barometer	Sea State		Sky Cond
Varia	Devia	True	Latitude	Longitude	Speed	RPM	Speed	Dir		Dir	Ft	

_____

Signed

NAUTICAL LOG

Date

From: _____   Towards: _____

Time	Course	Log	Comments	Watch Leader
0100				
0200				
0300				
0400				
0500				
0600				
0700				
0800				
0900				
1000				
1100				
1200				
1300				
1400				
1500				
1600				
1700				
1800				
1900				
2000				
2100				
2200				
2300				
2400				

Watches Set

Time	Leader	Crew	Time	Leader	Crew

NAUTICAL LOG

Constant Port: _____ 1st High Water: _____ 1st Low Water: _____

_____ 2nd High Water: _____ 2nd Low Water: _____

Local Port: _____ 1st High Water: _____ 1st Low Water: _____

_____ 2nd High Water: _____ 2nd Low Water: _____

M Compass			Position		Boat		Wind		Barometer	Sea State		Sky Cond
Varia	Devia	True	Latitude	Longitude	Speed	RPM	Speed	Dir		Dir	Ft	

_____

Signed

NAUTICAL LOG

Date

From: _____   Towards: _____

Time	Course	Log	Comments	Watch Leader
0100				
0200				
0300				
0400				
0500				
0600				
0700				
0800				
0900				
1000				
1100				
1200				
1300				
1400				
1500				
1600				
1700				
1800				
1900				
2000				
2100				
2200				
2300				
2400				

Watches Set

Time	Leader	Crew	Time	Leader	Crew

NAUTICAL LOG

Constant Port: _____ 1st High Water: _____ 1st Low Water: _____

_____ 2nd High Water: _____ 2nd Low Water: _____

Local Port: _____ 1st High Water: _____ 1st Low Water: _____

_____ 2nd High Water: _____ 2nd Low Water: _____

M Compass			Position		Boat		Wind		Barometer	Sea State		Sky Cond
Varia	Devia	True	Latitude	Longitude	Speed	RPM	Speed	Dir		Dir	Ft	

_____

Signed

NAUTICAL LOG

Date

From: _____   Towards: _____

Time	Course	Log	Comments	Watch Leader
0100				
0200				
0300				
0400				
0500				
0600				
0700				
0800				
0900				
1000				
1100				
1200				
1300				
1400				
1500				
1600				
1700				
1800				
1900				
2000				
2100				
2200				
2300				
2400				

Watches Set

Time	Leader	Crew	Time	Leader	Crew

NAUTICAL LOG

Constant Port: _____   1ˢᵗ High Water: _____   1ˢᵗ Low Water: _____

_____   2ⁿᵈ High Water: _____   2ⁿᵈ Low Water: _____

Local Port: _____   1ˢᵗ High Water: _____   1ˢᵗ Low Water: _____

_____   2ⁿᵈ High Water: _____   2ⁿᵈ Low Water: _____

M Compass			Position		Boat		Wind		Barometer	Sea State		Sky Cond
Varia	Devia	True	Latitude	Longitude	Speed	RPM	Speed	Dir		Dir	Ft	

_____
Signed

NAUTICAL LOG

Date

From: _____ Towards: _____

Time	Course	Log	Comments	Watch Leader
0100				
0200				
0300				
0400				
0500				
0600				
0700				
0800				
0900				
1000				
1100				
1200				
1300				
1400				
1500				
1600				
1700				
1800				
1900				
2000				
2100				
2200				
2300				
2400				

Watches Set

Time	Leader	Crew	Time	Leader	Crew

NAUTICAL LOG

Constant Port: _____   1st High Water: _____   1St Low Water: _____

_____   2nd High Water: _____   2nd Low Water: _____

Local Port: _____   1st High Water: _____   1st Low Water: _____

_____   2nd High Water: _____   2nd Low Water: _____

M Compass			Position		Boat		Wind		Barometer	Sea State		Sky Cond
Varia	Devia	True	Latitude	Longitude	Speed	RPM	Speed	Dir		Dir	Ft	

_____
Signed

NAUTICAL LOG

Date

From: _____   Towards: _____

Time	Course	Log	Comments	Watch Leader
0100				
0200				
0300				
0400				
0500				
0600				
0700				
0800				
0900				
1000				
1100				
1200				
1300				
1400				
1500				
1600				
1700				
1800				
1900				
2000				
2100				
2200				
2300				
2400				

Watches Set

Time	Leader	Crew	Time	Leader	Crew

NAUTICAL LOG

Constant Port: _____ 1st High Water: _____ 1st Low Water: _____

_____ 2nd High Water: _____ 2nd Low Water: _____

Local Port: _____ 1st High Water: _____ 1st Low Water: _____

_____ 2nd High Water: _____ 2nd Low Water: _____

M Compass			Position		Boat		Wind		Barometer	Sea State		Sky Cond
Varia	Devia	True	Latitude	Longitude	Speed	RPM	Speed	Dir		Dir	Ft	

_____

Signed

NAUTICAL LOG

Date

From: _____ Towards: _____

Time	Course	Log	Comments	Watch Leader
0100				
0200				
0300				
0400				
0500				
0600				
0700				
0800				
0900				
1000				
1100				
1200				
1300				
1400				
1500				
1600				
1700				
1800				
1900				
2000				
2100				
2200				
2300				
2400				

Watches Set

Time	Leader	Crew	Time	Leader	Crew

NAUTICAL LOG

Constant Port: _____   1st High Water: _____   1st Low Water: _____

                _____   2nd High Water: _____   2nd Low Water: _____

Local Port: _____   1st High Water: _____   1st Low Water: _____

                _____   2nd High Water: _____   2nd Low Water: _____

M Compass			Position		Boat		Wind		Barometer	Sea State		Sky Cond
Varia	Devia	True	Latitude	Longitude	Speed	RPM	Speed	Dir		Dir	Ft	

_____
Signed

NAUTICAL LOG

Date

From: _____   Towards: _____

Time	Course	Log	Comments	Watch Leader
0100				
0200				
0300				
0400				
0500				
0600				
0700				
0800				
0900				
1000				
1100				
1200				
1300				
1400				
1500				
1600				
1700				
1800				
1900				
2000				
2100				
2200				
2300				
2400				

Watches Set

Time	Leader	Crew	Time	Leader	Crew

NAUTICAL LOG

Constant Port: _____ 1st High Water: _____ 1st Low Water: _____

_____ 2nd High Water: _____ 2nd Low Water: _____

Local Port: _____ 1st High Water: _____ 1st Low Water: _____

_____ 2nd High Water: _____ 2nd Low Water: _____

M Compass			Position		Boat		Wind		Barometer	Sea State		Sky Cond
Varia	Devia	True	Latitude	Longitude	Speed	RPM	Speed	Dir		Dir	Ft	

_____

Signed

NAUTICAL LOG

Date

From: _____   Towards: _____

Time	Course	Log	Comments	Watch Leader
0100				
0200				
0300				
0400				
0500				
0600				
0700				
0800				
0900				
1000				
1100				
1200				
1300				
1400				
1500				
1600				
1700				
1800				
1900				
2000				
2100				
2200				
2300				
2400				

Watches Set

Time	Leader	Crew	Time	Leader	Crew

NAUTICAL LOG

Constant Port: _____   1ˢᵗ High Water: _____   1ˢᵗ Low Water: _____

_____   2ⁿᵈ High Water: _____   2ⁿᵈ Low Water: _____

Local Port: _____   1ˢᵗ High Water: _____   1ˢᵗ Low Water: _____

_____   2ⁿᵈ High Water: _____   2ⁿᵈ Low Water: _____

M Compass			Position		Boat		Wind		Barometer	Sea State		Sky Cond
Varia	Devia	True	Latitude	Longitude	Speed	RPM	Speed	Dir		Dir	Ft	

_____

Signed

NAUTICAL LOG

Date

From: _____   Towards: _____

Time	Course	Log	Comments	Watch Leader
0100				
0200				
0300				
0400				
0500				
0600				
0700				
0800				
0900				
1000				
1100				
1200				
1300				
1400				
1500				
1600				
1700				
1800				
1900				
2000				
2100				
2200				
2300				
2400				

Watches Set

Time	Leader	Crew	Time	Leader	Crew

NAUTICAL LOG

Constant Port: _____   1st High Water: _____   1st Low Water: _____

_____   2nd High Water: _____   2nd Low Water: _____

Local Port: _____   1st High Water: _____   1st Low Water: _____

_____   2nd High Water: _____   2nd Low Water: _____

M Compass			Position		Boat		Wind		Barometer	Sea State		Sky Cond
Varia	Devia	True	Latitude	Longitude	Speed	RPM	Speed	Dir		Dir	Ft	

_____
Signed

NAUTICAL LOG

Date

From: _____   Towards: _____

Time	Course	Log	Comments	Watch Leader
0100				
0200				
0300				
0400				
0500				
0600				
0700				
0800				
0900				
1000				
1100				
1200				
1300				
1400				
1500				
1600				
1700				
1800				
1900				
2000				
2100				
2200				
2300				
2400				

Watches Set

Time	Leader	Crew	Time	Leader	Crew

NAUTICAL LOG

Constant Port: _____   1st High Water: _____   1st Low Water: _____

_____   2nd High Water: _____   2nd Low Water: _____

Local Port: _____   1st High Water: _____   1st Low Water: _____

_____   2nd High Water: _____   2nd Low Water: _____

M Compass			Position		Boat		Wind		Barometer	Sea State		Sky Cond
Varia	Devia	True	Latitude	Longitude	Speed	RPM	Speed	Dir		Dir	Ft	

_____
Signed

NAUTICAL LOG

Date

From: _____   Towards: _____

Time	Course	Log	Comments	Watch Leader
0100				
0200				
0300				
0400				
0500				
0600				
0700				
0800				
0900				
1000				
1100				
1200				
1300				
1400				
1500				
1600				
1700				
1800				
1900				
2000				
2100				
2200				
2300				
2400				

Watches Set

Time	Leader	Crew	Time	Leader	Crew

NAUTICAL LOG

Constant Port: _____   1st High Water: _____   1st Low Water: _____

_____   2nd High Water: _____   2nd Low Water: _____

Local Port: _____   1st High Water: _____   1st Low Water: _____

_____   2nd High Water: _____   2nd Low Water: _____

M Compass			Position		Boat		Wind		Barometer	Sea State		Sky Cond
Varia	Devia	True	Latitude	Longitude	Speed	RPM	Speed	Dir		Dir	Ft	

_____
Signed

NAUTICAL LOG

Date

From: _____   Towards: _____

Time	Course	Log	Comments	Watch Leader
0100				
0200				
0300				
0400				
0500				
0600				
0700				
0800				
0900				
1000				
1100				
1200				
1300				
1400				
1500				
1600				
1700				
1800				
1900				
2000				
2100				
2200				
2300				
2400				

Watches Set

Time	Leader	Crew	Time	Leader	Crew

NAUTICAL LOG

Constant Port: _____ 1st High Water: _____ 1st Low Water: _____

_____ 2nd High Water: _____ 2nd Low Water: _____

Local Port: _____ 1st High Water: _____ 1st Low Water: _____

_____ 2nd High Water: _____ 2nd Low Water: _____

M Compass			Position		Boat		Wind		Barometer	Sea State		Sky Cond
Varia	Devia	True	Latitude	Longitude	Speed	RPM	Speed	Dir		Dir	Ft	

_____
Signed

NAUTICAL LOG

Date

From: _____   Towards: _____

Time	Course	Log	Comments	Watch Leader
0100				
0200				
0300				
0400				
0500				
0600				
0700				
0800				
0900				
1000				
1100				
1200				
1300				
1400				
1500				
1600				
1700				
1800				
1900				
2000				
2100				
2200				
2300				
2400				

Watches Set

Time	Leader	Crew	Time	Leader	Crew

NAUTICAL LOG

Constant Port: _____   1st High Water: _____   1st Low Water: _____

_____   2nd High Water: _____   2nd Low Water: _____

Local Port: _____   1st High Water: _____   1st Low Water: _____

_____   2nd High Water: _____   2nd Low Water: _____

M Compass			Position		Boat		Wind		Barometer	Sea State		Sky Cond
Varia	Devia	True	Latitude	Longitude	Speed	RPM	Speed	Dir		Dir	Ft	

_____
Signed

NAUTICAL LOG

Date

From: _____   Towards: _____

Time	Course	Log	Comments	Watch Leader
0100				
0200				
0300				
0400				
0500				
0600				
0700				
0800				
0900				
1000				
1100				
1200				
1300				
1400				
1500				
1600				
1700				
1800				
1900				
2000				
2100				
2200				
2300				
2400				

Watches Set

Time	Leader	Crew	Time	Leader	Crew

NAUTICAL LOG

Constant Port: _____   1st High Water: _____   1st Low Water: _____

_____   2nd High Water: _____   2nd Low Water: _____

Local Port: _____   1st High Water: _____   1st Low Water: _____

_____   2nd High Water: _____   2nd Low Water: _____

M Compass			Position		Boat		Wind		Barometer	Sea State		Sky Cond
Varia	Devia	True	Latitude	Longitude	Speed	RPM	Speed	Dir		Dir	Ft	

_____

Signed

NAUTICAL LOG

Date

From: _____   Towards: _____

Time	Course	Log	Comments	Watch Leader
0100				
0200				
0300				
0400				
0500				
0600				
0700				
0800				
0900				
1000				
1100				
1200				
1300				
1400				
1500				
1600				
1700				
1800				
1900				
2000				
2100				
2200				
2300				
2400				

Watches Set

Time	Leader	Crew	Time	Leader	Crew

NAUTICAL LOG

Constant Port: _____   1st High Water: _____   1st Low Water: _____

_____   2nd High Water: _____   2nd Low Water: _____

Local Port: _____   1st High Water: _____   1st Low Water: _____

_____   2nd High Water: _____   2nd Low Water: _____

M Compass			Position		Boat		Wind		Barometer	Sea State		Sky Cond
Varia	Devia	True	Latitude	Longitude	Speed	RPM	Speed	Dir		Dir	Ft	

_____

Signed

NAUTICAL LOG

Date

From: _____   Towards: _____

Time	Course	Log	Comments	Watch Leader
0100				
0200				
0300				
0400				
0500				
0600				
0700				
0800				
0900				
1000				
1100				
1200				
1300				
1400				
1500				
1600				
1700				
1800				
1900				
2000				
2100				
2200				
2300				
2400				

Watches Set

Time	Leader	Crew	Time	Leader	Crew

NAUTICAL LOG

Constant Port: _____   1st High Water: _____   1st Low Water: _____

_____   2nd High Water: _____   2nd Low Water: _____

Local Port: _____   1st High Water: _____   1st Low Water: _____

_____   2nd High Water: _____   2nd Low Water: _____

M Compass			Position		Boat		Wind		Barometer	Sea State		Sky Cond
Varia	Devia	True	Latitude	Longitude	Speed	RPM	Speed	Dir		Dir	Ft	

_____
Signed

NAUTICAL LOG

Date

From: _____   Towards: _____

Time	Course	Log	Comments	Watch Leader
0100				
0200				
0300				
0400				
0500				
0600				
0700				
0800				
0900				
1000				
1100				
1200				
1300				
1400				
1500				
1600				
1700				
1800				
1900				
2000				
2100				
2200				
2300				
2400				

Watches Set

Time	Leader	Crew	Time	Leader	Crew

NAUTICAL LOG

Constant Port: _____   1st High Water: _____   1st Low Water: _____

_____   2nd High Water: _____   2nd Low Water: _____

Local Port: _____   1st High Water: _____   1st Low Water: _____

_____   2nd High Water: _____   2nd Low Water: _____

M Compass			Position		Boat		Wind		Barometer	Sea State		Sky Cond
Varia	Devia	True	Latitude	Longitude	Speed	RPM	Speed	Dir		Dir	Ft	

_____
Signed

NAUTICAL LOG

Date

From: _____ Towards: _____

Time	Course	Log	Comments	Watch Leader
0100				
0200				
0300				
0400				
0500				
0600				
0700				
0800				
0900				
1000				
1100				
1200				
1300				
1400				
1500				
1600				
1700				
1800				
1900				
2000				
2100				
2200				
2300				
2400				

Watches Set

Time	Leader	Crew	Time	Leader	Crew

NAUTICAL LOG

Constant Port: _____ 1st High Water: _____ 1st Low Water: _____

_____ 2nd High Water: _____ 2nd Low Water: _____

Local Port: _____ 1st High Water: _____ 1st Low Water: _____

_____ 2nd High Water: _____ 2nd Low Water: _____

M Compass			Position		Boat		Wind		Barometer	Sea State		Sky Cond
Varia	Devia	True	Latitude	Longitude	Speed	RPM	Speed	Dir		Dir	Ft	

_____
Signed

NAUTICAL LOG

Date

From: _____   Towards: _____

Time	Course	Log	Comments	Watch Leader
0100				
0200				
0300				
0400				
0500				
0600				
0700				
0800				
0900				
1000				
1100				
1200				
1300				
1400				
1500				
1600				
1700				
1800				
1900				
2000				
2100				
2200				
2300				
2400				

Watches Set

Time	Leader	Crew	Time	Leader	Crew

NAUTICAL LOG

Constant Port: _____   1ˢᵗ High Water: _____   1ˢᵗ Low Water: _____

_____   2ⁿᵈ High Water: _____   2ⁿᵈ Low Water: _____

Local Port: _____   1ˢᵗ High Water: _____   1ˢᵗ Low Water: _____

_____   2ⁿᵈ High Water: _____   2ⁿᵈ Low Water: _____

M Compass			Position		Boat		Wind		Barometer	Sea State		Sky Cond
Varia	Devia	True	Latitude	Longitude	Speed	RPM	Speed	Dir		Dir	Ft	

_____

Signed

NAUTICAL LOG

Date

From: _____ Towards: _____

Time	Course	Log	Comments	Watch Leader
0100				
0200				
0300				
0400				
0500				
0600				
0700				
0800				
0900				
1000				
1100				
1200				
1300				
1400				
1500				
1600				
1700				
1800				
1900				
2000				
2100				
2200				
2300				
2400				

Watches Set

Time	Leader	Crew	Time	Leader	Crew

NAUTICAL LOG

Constant Port: _____   1ˢᵗ High Water: _____   1ˢᵗ Low Water: _____

_____   2ⁿᵈ High Water: _____   2ⁿᵈ Low Water: _____

Local Port: _____   1ˢᵗ High Water: _____   1ˢᵗ Low Water: _____

_____   2ⁿᵈ High Water: _____   2ⁿᵈ Low Water: _____

M Compass			Position		Boat		Wind		Barometer	Sea State		Sky Cond
Varia	Devia	True	Latitude	Longitude	Speed	RPM	Speed	Dir		Dir	Ft	

_____

Signed

NAUTICAL LOG

Date

From: _____   Towards: _____

Time	Course	Log	Comments	Watch Leader
0100				
0200				
0300				
0400				
0500				
0600				
0700				
0800				
0900				
1000				
1100				
1200				
1300				
1400				
1500				
1600				
1700				
1800				
1900				
2000				
2100				
2200				
2300				
2400				

Watches Set

Time	Leader	Crew	Time	Leader	Crew

NAUTICAL LOG

Constant Port: _____   1st High Water: _____   1st Low Water: _____

_____   2nd High Water: _____   2nd Low Water: _____

Local Port: _____   1st High Water: _____   1st Low Water: _____

_____   2nd High Water: _____   2nd Low Water: _____

M Compass			Position		Boat		Wind		Barometer	Sea State		Sky Cond
Varia	Devia	True	Latitude	Longitude	Speed	RPM	Speed	Dir		Dir	Ft	

_____
Signed

NAUTICAL LOG

Date

From: _____   Towards: _____

Time	Course	Log	Comments	Watch Leader
0100				
0200				
0300				
0400				
0500				
0600				
0700				
0800				
0900				
1000				
1100				
1200				
1300				
1400				
1500				
1600				
1700				
1800				
1900				
2000				
2100				
2200				
2300				
2400				

Watches Set

Time	Leader	Crew	Time	Leader	Crew

NAUTICAL LOG

Constant Port: _____ 1st High Water: _____ 1st Low Water: _____

_____ 2nd High Water: _____ 2nd Low Water: _____

Local Port: _____ 1st High Water: _____ 1st Low Water: _____

_____ 2nd High Water: _____ 2nd Low Water: _____

M Compass			Position		Boat		Wind		Barometer	Sea State		Sky Cond
Varia	Devia	True	Latitude	Longitude	Speed	RPM	Speed	Dir		Dir	Ft	

_____

Signed

NAUTICAL LOG

Date

From: _____   Towards: _____

Time	Course	Log	Comments	Watch Leader
0100				
0200				
0300				
0400				
0500				
0600				
0700				
0800				
0900				
1000				
1100				
1200				
1300				
1400				
1500				
1600				
1700				
1800				
1900				
2000				
2100				
2200				
2300				
2400				

Watches Set

Time	Leader	Crew	Time	Leader	Crew

NAUTICAL LOG

Constant Port: _____   1st High Water: _____   1st Low Water: _____

_____   2nd High Water: _____   2nd Low Water: _____

Local Port: _____   1st High Water: _____   1st Low Water: _____

_____   2nd High Water: _____   2nd Low Water: _____

M Compass			Position		Boat		Wind		Barometer	Sea State		Sky Cond
Varia	Devia	True	Latitude	Longitude	Speed	RPM	Speed	Dir		Dir	Ft	

_____

Signed

NAUTICAL LOG

Date

From: _____   Towards: _____

Time	Course	Log	Comments	Watch Leader
0100				
0200				
0300				
0400				
0500				
0600				
0700				
0800				
0900				
1000				
1100				
1200				
1300				
1400				
1500				
1600				
1700				
1800				
1900				
2000				
2100				
2200				
2300				
2400				

Watches Set

Time	Leader	Crew	Time	Leader	Crew

NAUTICAL LOG

Constant Port: _____   1st High Water: _____   1st Low Water: _____

_____   2nd High Water: _____   2nd Low Water: _____

Local Port: _____   1st High Water: _____   1st Low Water: _____

_____   2nd High Water: _____   2nd Low Water: _____

M Compass			Position		Boat		Wind		Barometer	Sea State		Sky Cond
Varia	Devia	True	Latitude	Longitude	Speed	RPM	Speed	Dir		Dir	Ft	

_____
Signed

NAUTICAL LOG

Date

From: _____   Towards: _____

Time	Course	Log	Comments	Watch Leader
0100				
0200				
0300				
0400				
0500				
0600				
0700				
0800				
0900				
1000				
1100				
1200				
1300				
1400				
1500				
1600				
1700				
1800				
1900				
2000				
2100				
2200				
2300				
2400				

Watches Set

Time	Leader	Crew	Time	Leader	Crew

NAUTICAL LOG

Constant Port: _____   1st High Water: _____   1st Low Water: _____

_____   2nd High Water: _____   2nd Low Water: _____

Local Port: _____   1st High Water: _____   1st Low Water: _____

_____   2nd High Water: _____   2nd Low Water: _____

M Compass			Position		Boat		Wind		Barometer	Sea State		Sky Cond
Varia	Devia	True	Latitude	Longitude	Speed	RPM	Speed	Dir		Dir	Ft	

_____
Signed

NAUTICAL LOG

Date

From: _____   Towards: _____

Time	Course	Log	Comments	Watch Leader
0100				
0200				
0300				
0400				
0500				
0600				
0700				
0800				
0900				
1000				
1100				
1200				
1300				
1400				
1500				
1600				
1700				
1800				
1900				
2000				
2100				
2200				
2300				
2400				

Watches Set

Time	Leader	Crew	Time	Leader	Crew

NAUTICAL LOG

Constant Port: _____   1ˢᵗ High Water: _____   1ˢᵗ Low Water: _____

_____   2ⁿᵈ High Water: _____   2ⁿᵈ Low Water: _____

Local Port: _____   1ˢᵗ High Water: _____   1ˢᵗ Low Water: _____

_____   2ⁿᵈ High Water: _____   2ⁿᵈ Low Water: _____

M Compass			Position		Boat		Wind		Barometer	Sea State		Sky Cond
Varia	Devia	True	Latitude	Longitude	Speed	RPM	Speed	Dir		Dir	Ft	

_____

Signed

NAUTICAL LOG

Date

From: _____   Towards: _____

Time	Course	Log	Comments	Watch Leader
0100				
0200				
0300				
0400				
0500				
0600				
0700				
0800				
0900				
1000				
1100				
1200				
1300				
1400				
1500				
1600				
1700				
1800				
1900				
2000				
2100				
2200				
2300				
2400				

Watches Set

Time	Leader	Crew	Time	Leader	Crew

NAUTICAL LOG

Constant Port: _____ 1st High Water: _____ 1st Low Water: _____

_____ 2nd High Water: _____ 2nd Low Water: _____

Local Port: _____ 1st High Water: _____ 1st Low Water: _____

_____ 2nd High Water: _____ 2nd Low Water: _____

M Compass			Position		Boat		Wind		Barometer	Sea State		Sky Cond
Varia	Devia	True	Latitude	Longitude	Speed	RPM	Speed	Dir		Dir	Ft	

_____
Signed

NAUTICAL LOG

Date

From: _____   Towards: _____

Time	Course	Log	Comments	Watch Leader
0100				
0200				
0300				
0400				
0500				
0600				
0700				
0800				
0900				
1000				
1100				
1200				
1300				
1400				
1500				
1600				
1700				
1800				
1900				
2000				
2100				
2200				
2300				
2400				

Watches Set

Time	Leader	Crew	Time	Leader	Crew

NAUTICAL LOG

Constant Port: _____　　1st High Water: _____　　1st Low Water: _____

_____　　2nd High Water: _____　　2nd Low Water: _____

Local Port: _____　　1st High Water: _____　　1st Low Water: _____

_____　　2nd High Water: _____　　2nd Low Water: _____

M Compass			Position		Boat		Wind		Barometer	Sea State		Sky Cond
Varia	Devia	True	Latitude	Longitude	Speed	RPM	Speed	Dir		Dir	Ft	

_____

Signed

NAUTICAL LOG

Date

From: _____   Towards: _____

Time	Course	Log	Comments	Watch Leader
0100				
0200				
0300				
0400				
0500				
0600				
0700				
0800				
0900				
1000				
1100				
1200				
1300				
1400				
1500				
1600				
1700				
1800				
1900				
2000				
2100				
2200				
2300				
2400				

Watches Set

Time	Leader	Crew	Time	Leader	Crew

NAUTICAL LOG

Constant Port: _____   1st High Water: _____   1st Low Water: _____

_____   2nd High Water: _____   2nd Low Water: _____

Local Port: _____   1st High Water: _____   1st Low Water: _____

_____   2nd High Water: _____   2nd Low Water: _____

M Compass			Position		Boat		Wind		Barometer	Sea State		Sky Cond
Varia	Devia	True	Latitude	Longitude	Speed	RPM	Speed	Dir		Dir	Ft	

_____
Signed

NAUTICAL LOG

Date

From: _____   Towards: _____

Time	Course	Log	Comments	Watch Leader
0100				
0200				
0300				
0400				
0500				
0600				
0700				
0800				
0900				
1000				
1100				
1200				
1300				
1400				
1500				
1600				
1700				
1800				
1900				
2000				
2100				
2200				
2300				
2400				

Watches Set

Time	Leader	Crew	Time	Leader	Crew

NAUTICAL LOG

Constant Port: _____   1st High Water: _____   1st Low Water: _____

_____   2nd High Water: _____   2nd Low Water: _____

Local Port: _____   1st High Water: _____   1st Low Water: _____

_____   2nd High Water: _____   2nd Low Water: _____

M Compass			Position		Boat		Wind		Barometer	Sea State		Sky Cond
Varia	Devia	True	Latitude	Longitude	Speed	RPM	Speed	Dir		Dir	Ft	

_____
Signed

NAUTICAL LOG

Date

From: _____   Towards: _____

Time	Course	Log	Comments	Watch Leader
0100				
0200				
0300				
0400				
0500				
0600				
0700				
0800				
0900				
1000				
1100				
1200				
1300				
1400				
1500				
1600				
1700				
1800				
1900				
2000				
2100				
2200				
2300				
2400				

Watches Set

Time	Leader	Crew	Time	Leader	Crew

NAUTICAL LOG

Constant Port: _____   1st High Water: _____   1st Low Water: _____

_____   2nd High Water: _____   2nd Low Water: _____

Local Port: _____   1st High Water: _____   1st Low Water: _____

_____   2nd High Water: _____   2nd Low Water: _____

M Compass			Position		Boat		Wind		Barometer	Sea State		Sky Cond
Varia	Devia	True	Latitude	Longitude	Speed	RPM	Speed	Dir		Dir	Ft	

_____
Signed

NAUTICAL LOG

Date

From: _____   Towards: _____

Time	Course	Log	Comments	Watch Leader
0100				
0200				
0300				
0400				
0500				
0600				
0700				
0800				
0900				
1000				
1100				
1200				
1300				
1400				
1500				
1600				
1700				
1800				
1900				
2000				
2100				
2200				
2300				
2400				

Watches Set

Time	Leader	Crew	Time	Leader	Crew

NAUTICAL LOG

Constant Port: _____   1st High Water: _____   1st Low Water: _____

_____   2nd High Water: _____   2nd Low Water: _____

Local Port: _____   1st High Water: _____   1st Low Water: _____

_____   2nd High Water: _____   2nd Low Water: _____

M Compass			Position		Boat		Wind		Barometer	Sea State		Sky Cond
Varia	Devia	True	Latitude	Longitude	Speed	RPM	Speed	Dir		Dir	Ft	

_____
Signed

NAUTICAL LOG

Date

From: _____ Towards: _____

Time	Course	Log	Comments	Watch Leader
0100				
0200				
0300				
0400				
0500				
0600				
0700				
0800				
0900				
1000				
1100				
1200				
1300				
1400				
1500				
1600				
1700				
1800				
1900				
2000				
2100				
2200				
2300				
2400				

Watches Set

Time	Leader	Crew	Time	Leader	Crew

NAUTICAL LOG

Constant Port: _____ 1st High Water: _____ 1st Low Water: _____

_____ 2nd High Water: _____ 2nd Low Water: _____

Local Port: _____ 1st High Water: _____ 1st Low Water: _____

_____ 2nd High Water: _____ 2nd Low Water: _____

M Compass			Position		Boat		Wind		Barometer	Sea State		Sky Cond
Varia	Devia	True	Latitude	Longitude	Speed	RPM	Speed	Dir		Dir	Ft	

_____
Signed

NAUTICAL LOG

Date

From: _____ Towards: _____

Time	Course	Log	Comments	Watch Leader
0100				
0200				
0300				
0400				
0500				
0600				
0700				
0800				
0900				
1000				
1100				
1200				
1300				
1400				
1500				
1600				
1700				
1800				
1900				
2000				
2100				
2200				
2300				
2400				

Watches Set

Time	Leader	Crew	Time	Leader	Crew

NAUTICAL LOG

Constant Port: _____   1st High Water: _____   1st Low Water: _____

_____   2nd High Water: _____   2nd Low Water: _____

Local Port: _____   1st High Water: _____   1st Low Water: _____

_____   2nd High Water: _____   2nd Low Water: _____

M Compass			Position		Boat		Wind		Barometer	Sea State		Sky Cond
Varia	Devia	True	Latitude	Longitude	Speed	RPM	Speed	Dir		Dir	Ft	

_____
Signed

NAUTICAL LOG

Date

From: _____   Towards: _____

Time	Course	Log	Comments	Watch Leader
0100				
0200				
0300				
0400				
0500				
0600				
0700				
0800				
0900				
1000				
1100				
1200				
1300				
1400				
1500				
1600				
1700				
1800				
1900				
2000				
2100				
2200				
2300				
2400				

Watches Set

Time	Leader	Crew	Time	Leader	Crew

NAUTICAL LOG

Constant Port: _____ 1st High Water: _____ 1st Low Water: _____

_____ 2nd High Water: _____ 2nd Low Water: _____

Local Port: _____ 1st High Water: _____ 1st Low Water: _____

_____ 2nd High Water: _____ 2nd Low Water: _____

M Compass			Position		Boat		Wind		Barometer	Sea State		Sky Cond
Varia	Devia	True	Latitude	Longitude	Speed	RPM	Speed	Dir		Dir	Ft	

_____
Signed

NAUTICAL LOG

Date

From: _____   Towards: _____

Time	Course	Log	Comments	Watch Leader
0100				
0200				
0300				
0400				
0500				
0600				
0700				
0800				
0900				
1000				
1100				
1200				
1300				
1400				
1500				
1600				
1700				
1800				
1900				
2000				
2100				
2200				
2300				
2400				

Watches Set

Time	Leader	Crew	Time	Leader	Crew

NAUTICAL LOG

Constant Port: _____ 1ˢᵗ High Water: _____ 1ˢᵗ Low Water: _____

_____ 2ⁿᵈ High Water: _____ 2ⁿᵈ Low Water: _____

Local Port: _____ 1ˢᵗ High Water: _____ 1ˢᵗ Low Water: _____

_____ 2ⁿᵈ High Water: _____ 2ⁿᵈ Low Water: _____

M Compass			Position		Boat		Wind		Barometer	Sea State		Sky Cond
Varia	Devia	True	Latitude	Longitude	Speed	RPM	Speed	Dir		Dir	Ft	

_____

Signed

NAUTICAL LOG

Date

From: _____   Towards: _____

Time	Course	Log	Comments	Watch Leader
0100				
0200				
0300				
0400				
0500				
0600				
0700				
0800				
0900				
1000				
1100				
1200				
1300				
1400				
1500				
1600				
1700				
1800				
1900				
2000				
2100				
2200				
2300				
2400				

Watches Set

Time	Leader	Crew	Time	Leader	Crew

NAUTICAL LOG

Constant Port: _____   1st High Water: _____   1st Low Water: _____

_____   2nd High Water: _____   2nd Low Water: _____

Local Port: _____   1st High Water: _____   1st Low Water: _____

_____   2nd High Water: _____   2nd Low Water: _____

M Compass			Position		Boat		Wind		Barometer	Sea State		Sky Cond
Varia	Devia	True	Latitude	Longitude	Speed	RPM	Speed	Dir		Dir	Ft	

_____
Signed

NAUTICAL LOG

Date

From: _____   Towards: _____

Time	Course	Log	Comments	Watch Leader
0100				
0200				
0300				
0400				
0500				
0600				
0700				
0800				
0900				
1000				
1100				
1200				
1300				
1400				
1500				
1600				
1700				
1800				
1900				
2000				
2100				
2200				
2300				
2400				

Watches Set

Time	Leader	Crew	Time	Leader	Crew

NAUTICAL LOG

Constant Port: _____   1st High Water: _____   1St Low Water: _____

_____   2nd High Water: _____   2nd Low Water: _____

Local Port: _____   1st High Water: _____   1st Low Water: _____

_____   2nd High Water: _____   2nd Low Water: _____

M Compass			Position		Boat		Wind		Barometer	Sea State		Sky Cond
Varia	Devia	True	Latitude	Longitude	Speed	RPM	Speed	Dir		Dir	Ft	

_____

Signed

NAUTICAL LOG

Date

From: _____   Towards: _____

Time	Course	Log	Comments	Watch Leader
0100				
0200				
0300				
0400				
0500				
0600				
0700				
0800				
0900				
1000				
1100				
1200				
1300				
1400				
1500				
1600				
1700				
1800				
1900				
2000				
2100				
2200				
2300				
2400				

Watches Set

Time	Leader	Crew	Time	Leader	Crew

NAUTICAL LOG

Constant Port: _____   1st High Water: _____   1st Low Water: _____

_____   2nd High Water: _____   2nd Low Water: _____

Local Port: _____   1st High Water: _____   1st Low Water: _____

_____   2nd High Water: _____   2nd Low Water: _____

M Compass			Position		Boat		Wind		Barometer	Sea State		Sky Cond
Varia	Devia	True	Latitude	Longitude	Speed	RPM	Speed	Dir		Dir	Ft	

_____

Signed

NAUTICAL LOG

Date

From: _____   Towards: _____

Time	Course	Log	Comments	Watch Leader
0100				
0200				
0300				
0400				
0500				
0600				
0700				
0800				
0900				
1000				
1100				
1200				
1300				
1400				
1500				
1600				
1700				
1800				
1900				
2000				
2100				
2200				
2300				
2400				

Watches Set

Time	Leader	Crew	Time	Leader	Crew

NAUTICAL LOG

Constant Port: _____   1st High Water: _____   1st Low Water: _____

_____   2nd High Water: _____   2nd Low Water: _____

Local Port: _____   1st High Water: _____   1st Low Water: _____

_____   2nd High Water: _____   2nd Low Water: _____

M Compass			Position		Boat		Wind		Barometer	Sea State		Sky Cond
Varia	Devia	True	Latitude	Longitude	Speed	RPM	Speed	Dir		Dir	Ft	

_____
Signed

NAUTICAL LOG

Date

From: _____   Towards: _____

Time	Course	Log	Comments	Watch Leader
0100				
0200				
0300				
0400				
0500				
0600				
0700				
0800				
0900				
1000				
1100				
1200				
1300				
1400				
1500				
1600				
1700				
1800				
1900				
2000				
2100				
2200				
2300				
2400				

Watches Set

Time	Leader	Crew	Time	Leader	Crew

NAUTICAL LOG

Constant Port: _____ 1st High Water: _____ 1st Low Water: _____

_____ 2nd High Water: _____ 2nd Low Water: _____

Local Port: _____ 1st High Water: _____ 1st Low Water: _____

_____ 2nd High Water: _____ 2nd Low Water: _____

M Compass			Position		Boat		Wind		Barometer	Sea State		Sky Cond
Varia	Devia	True	Latitude	Longitude	Speed	RPM	Speed	Dir		Dir	Ft	

_____
Signed

NAUTICAL LOG

Date

From: _____   Towards: _____

Time	Course	Log	Comments	Watch Leader
0100				
0200				
0300				
0400				
0500				
0600				
0700				
0800				
0900				
1000				
1100				
1200				
1300				
1400				
1500				
1600				
1700				
1800				
1900				
2000				
2100				
2200				
2300				
2400				

Watches Set

Time	Leader	Crew	Time	Leader	Crew

NAUTICAL LOG

Constant Port: _____   1st High Water: _____   1st Low Water: _____

_____   2nd High Water: _____   2nd Low Water: _____

Local Port: _____   1st High Water: _____   1st Low Water: _____

_____   2nd High Water: _____   2nd Low Water: _____

M Compass			Position		Boat		Wind		Barometer	Sea State		Sky Cond
Varia	Devia	True	Latitude	Longitude	Speed	RPM	Speed	Dir		Dir	Ft	

_____

Signed

NAUTICAL LOG

Date

From: _____   Towards: _____

Time	Course	Log	Comments	Watch Leader
0100				
0200				
0300				
0400				
0500				
0600				
0700				
0800				
0900				
1000				
1100				
1200				
1300				
1400				
1500				
1600				
1700				
1800				
1900				
2000				
2100				
2200				
2300				
2400				

Watches Set

Time	Leader	Crew	Time	Leader	Crew

NAUTICAL LOG

Constant Port: _____   1ˢᵗ High Water: _____   1ˢᵗ Low Water: _____

_____   2ⁿᵈ High Water: _____   2ⁿᵈ Low Water: _____

Local Port: _____   1ˢᵗ High Water: _____   1ˢᵗ Low Water: _____

_____   2ⁿᵈ High Water: _____   2ⁿᵈ Low Water: _____

M Compass			Position		Boat		Wind		Barometer	Sea State		Sky Cond
Varia	Devia	True	Latitude	Longitude	Speed	RPM	Speed	Dir		Dir	Ft	

_____

Signed

NAUTICAL LOG

Date

From: _____   Towards: _____

Time	Course	Log	Comments	Watch Leader
0100				
0200				
0300				
0400				
0500				
0600				
0700				
0800				
0900				
1000				
1100				
1200				
1300				
1400				
1500				
1600				
1700				
1800				
1900				
2000				
2100				
2200				
2300				
2400				

Watches Set

Time	Leader	Crew	Time	Leader	Crew

NAUTICAL LOG

Constant Port: _____ 1ˢᵗ High Water: _____ 1ˢᵗ Low Water: _____

_____ 2ⁿᵈ High Water: _____ 2ⁿᵈ Low Water: _____

Local Port: _____ 1ˢᵗ High Water: _____ 1ˢᵗ Low Water: _____

_____ 2ⁿᵈ High Water: _____ 2ⁿᵈ Low Water: _____

M Compass			Position		Boat		Wind		Barometer	Sea State		Sky Cond
Varia	Devia	True	Latitude	Longitude	Speed	RPM	Speed	Dir		Dir	Ft	

_____

Signed

NAUTICAL LOG

Date

From: _____   Towards: _____

Time	Course	Log	Comments	Watch Leader
0100				
0200				
0300				
0400				
0500				
0600				
0700				
0800				
0900				
1000				
1100				
1200				
1300				
1400				
1500				
1600				
1700				
1800				
1900				
2000				
2100				
2200				
2300				
2400				

Watches Set

Time	Leader	Crew	Time	Leader	Crew

NAUTICAL LOG

Constant Port: _____   1ˢᵗ High Water: _____   1ˢᵗ Low Water: _____

_____   2ⁿᵈ High Water: _____   2ⁿᵈ Low Water: _____

Local Port: _____   1ˢᵗ High Water: _____   1ˢᵗ Low Water: _____

_____   2ⁿᵈ High Water: _____   2ⁿᵈ Low Water: _____

M Compass			Position		Boat		Wind		Barometer	Sea State		Sky Cond
Varia	Devia	True	Latitude	Longitude	Speed	RPM	Speed	Dir		Dir	Ft	

_____
Signed

NAUTICAL LOG

Date

From: _____   Towards: _____

Time	Course	Log	Comments	Watch Leader
0100				
0200				
0300				
0400				
0500				
0600				
0700				
0800				
0900				
1000				
1100				
1200				
1300				
1400				
1500				
1600				
1700				
1800				
1900				
2000				
2100				
2200				
2300				
2400				

Watches Set

Time	Leader	Crew	Time	Leader	Crew

NAUTICAL LOG

Constant Port: _____   1st High Water: _____   1st Low Water: _____

_____   2nd High Water: _____   2nd Low Water: _____

Local Port: _____   1st High Water: _____   1st Low Water: _____

_____   2nd High Water: _____   2nd Low Water: _____

M Compass			Position		Boat		Wind		Barometer	Sea State		Sky Cond
Varia	Devia	True	Latitude	Longitude	Speed	RPM	Speed	Dir		Dir	Ft	

_____
Signed

NAUTICAL LOG

Date

From: _____   Towards: _____

Time	Course	Log	Comments	Watch Leader
0100				
0200				
0300				
0400				
0500				
0600				
0700				
0800				
0900				
1000				
1100				
1200				
1300				
1400				
1500				
1600				
1700				
1800				
1900				
2000				
2100				
2200				
2300				
2400				

Watches Set

Time	Leader	Crew	Time	Leader	Crew

NAUTICAL LOG

Constant Port: _____   1st High Water: _____   1st Low Water: _____

_____   2nd High Water: _____   2nd Low Water: _____

Local Port: _____   1st High Water: _____   1st Low Water: _____

_____   2nd High Water: _____   2nd Low Water: _____

M Compass			Position		Boat		Wind		Barometer	Sea State		Sky Cond
Varia	Devia	True	Latitude	Longitude	Speed	RPM	Speed	Dir		Dir	Ft	

_____

Signed

NAUTICAL LOG

Date

From: _____ Towards: _____

Time	Course	Log	Comments	Watch Leader
0100				
0200				
0300				
0400				
0500				
0600				
0700				
0800				
0900				
1000				
1100				
1200				
1300				
1400				
1500				
1600				
1700				
1800				
1900				
2000				
2100				
2200				
2300				
2400				

Watches Set

Time	Leader	Crew	Time	Leader	Crew

NAUTICAL LOG

Constant Port: _____   1st High Water: _____   1st Low Water: _____

_____   2nd High Water: _____   2nd Low Water: _____

Local Port: _____   1st High Water: _____   1st Low Water: _____

_____   2nd High Water: _____   2nd Low Water: _____

M Compass			Position		Boat		Wind		Barometer	Sea State		Sky Cond
Varia	Devia	True	Latitude	Longitude	Speed	RPM	Speed	Dir		Dir	Ft	

_____
Signed

NAUTICAL LOG

Date

From: _____   Towards: _____

Time	Course	Log	Comments	Watch Leader
0100				
0200				
0300				
0400				
0500				
0600				
0700				
0800				
0900				
1000				
1100				
1200				
1300				
1400				
1500				
1600				
1700				
1800				
1900				
2000				
2100				
2200				
2300				
2400				

Watches Set

Time	Leader	Crew	Time	Leader	Crew

NAUTICAL LOG

Constant Port: _____   1st High Water: _____   1st Low Water: _____

_____   2nd High Water: _____   2nd Low Water: _____

Local Port: _____   1st High Water: _____   1st Low Water: _____

_____   2nd High Water: _____   2nd Low Water: _____

M Compass			Position		Boat		Wind		Barometer	Sea State		Sky Cond
Varia	Devia	True	Latitude	Longitude	Speed	RPM	Speed	Dir		Dir	Ft	

_____

Signed

NAUTICAL LOG

Date

From: _____   Towards: _____

Time	Course	Log	Comments	Watch Leader
0100				
0200				
0300				
0400				
0500				
0600				
0700				
0800				
0900				
1000				
1100				
1200				
1300				
1400				
1500				
1600				
1700				
1800				
1900				
2000				
2100				
2200				
2300				
2400				

Watches Set

Time	Leader	Crew	Time	Leader	Crew

NAUTICAL LOG

Constant Port: _____   1st High Water: _____   1st Low Water: _____

_____   2nd High Water: _____   2nd Low Water: _____

Local Port: _____   1st High Water: _____   1st Low Water: _____

_____   2nd High Water: _____   2nd Low Water: _____

M Compass			Position		Boat		Wind		Barometer	Sea State		Sky Cond
Varia	Devia	True	Latitude	Longitude	Speed	RPM	Speed	Dir		Dir	Ft	

_____

Signed

NAUTICAL LOG

Date

From: _____   Towards: _____

Time	Course	Log	Comments	Watch Leader
0100				
0200				
0300				
0400				
0500				
0600				
0700				
0800				
0900				
1000				
1100				
1200				
1300				
1400				
1500				
1600				
1700				
1800				
1900				
2000				
2100				
2200				
2300				
2400				

Watches Set

Time	Leader	Crew	Time	Leader	Crew

NAUTICAL LOG

Constant Port: _____ 1ˢᵗ High Water: _____ 1ˢᵗ Low Water: _____

_____ 2ⁿᵈ High Water: _____ 2ⁿᵈ Low Water: _____

Local Port: _____ 1ˢᵗ High Water: _____ 1ˢᵗ Low Water: _____

_____ 2ⁿᵈ High Water: _____ 2ⁿᵈ Low Water: _____

M Compass			Position		Boat		Wind		Barometer	Sea State		Sky Cond
Varia	Devia	True	Latitude	Longitude	Speed	RPM	Speed	Dir		Dir	Ft	

_____

Signed

NAUTICAL LOG

Date

From: _____   Towards: _____

Time	Course	Log	Comments	Watch Leader
0100				
0200				
0300				
0400				
0500				
0600				
0700				
0800				
0900				
1000				
1100				
1200				
1300				
1400				
1500				
1600				
1700				
1800				
1900				
2000				
2100				
2200				
2300				
2400				

Watches Set

Time	Leader	Crew	Time	Leader	Crew

NAUTICAL LOG

Constant Port: _____   1st High Water: _____   1st Low Water: _____

_____   2nd High Water: _____   2nd Low Water: _____

Local Port: _____   1st High Water: _____   1st Low Water: _____

_____   2nd High Water: _____   2nd Low Water: _____

M Compass			Position		Boat		Wind		Barometer	Sea State		Sky Cond
Varia	Devia	True	Latitude	Longitude	Speed	RPM	Speed	Dir		Dir	Ft	

_____

Signed

NAUTICAL LOG

Date

From: _____   Towards: _____

Time	Course	Log	Comments	Watch Leader
0100				
0200				
0300				
0400				
0500				
0600				
0700				
0800				
0900				
1000				
1100				
1200				
1300				
1400				
1500				
1600				
1700				
1800				
1900				
2000				
2100				
2200				
2300				
2400				

Watches Set

Time	Leader	Crew	Time	Leader	Crew

NAUTICAL LOG

Constant Port: _____   1st High Water: _____   1st Low Water: _____

_____   2nd High Water: _____   2nd Low Water: _____

Local Port: _____   1st High Water: _____   1st Low Water: _____

_____   2nd High Water: _____   2nd Low Water: _____

M Compass			Position		Boat		Wind		Barometer	Sea State		Sky Cond
Varia	Devia	True	Latitude	Longitude	Speed	RPM	Speed	Dir		Dir	Ft	

_____
Signed

NAUTICAL LOG

Date

From: _____   Towards: _____

Time	Course	Log	Comments	Watch Leader
0100				
0200				
0300				
0400				
0500				
0600				
0700				
0800				
0900				
1000				
1100				
1200				
1300				
1400				
1500				
1600				
1700				
1800				
1900				
2000				
2100				
2200				
2300				
2400				

Watches Set

Time	Leader	Crew	Time	Leader	Crew

NAUTICAL LOG

Constant Port: _____   1st High Water: _____   1st Low Water: _____

_____   2nd High Water: _____   2nd Low Water: _____

Local Port: _____   1st High Water: _____   1st Low Water: _____

_____   2nd High Water: _____   2nd Low Water: _____

M Compass			Position		Boat		Wind		Barometer	Sea State		Sky Cond
Varia	Devia	True	Latitude	Longitude	Speed	RPM	Speed	Dir		Dir	Ft	

_____

Signed

NAUTICAL LOG

Date

From: _____   Towards: _____

Time	Course	Log	Comments	Watch Leader
0100				
0200				
0300				
0400				
0500				
0600				
0700				
0800				
0900				
1000				
1100				
1200				
1300				
1400				
1500				
1600				
1700				
1800				
1900				
2000				
2100				
2200				
2300				
2400				

Watches Set

Time	Leader	Crew	Time	Leader	Crew

NAUTICAL LOG

Constant Port: _____   1st High Water: _____   1st Low Water: _____

_____   2nd High Water: _____   2nd Low Water: _____

Local Port: _____   1st High Water: _____   1st Low Water: _____

_____   2nd High Water: _____   2nd Low Water: _____

M Compass			Position		Boat		Wind		Barometer	Sea State		Sky Cond
Varia	Devia	True	Latitude	Longitude	Speed	RPM	Speed	Dir		Dir	Ft	

_____
Signed

NAUTICAL LOG

Date

From: _____ Towards: _____

Time	Course	Log	Comments	Watch Leader
0100				
0200				
0300				
0400				
0500				
0600				
0700				
0800				
0900				
1000				
1100				
1200				
1300				
1400				
1500				
1600				
1700				
1800				
1900				
2000				
2100				
2200				
2300				
2400				

Watches Set

Time	Leader	Crew	Time	Leader	Crew

NAUTICAL LOG

Constant Port: _____   1st High Water: _____   1st Low Water: _____

_____   2nd High Water: _____   2nd Low Water: _____

Local Port: _____   1st High Water: _____   1st Low Water: _____

_____   2nd High Water: _____   2nd Low Water: _____

M Compass			Position		Boat		Wind		Barometer	Sea State		Sky Cond
Varia	Devia	True	Latitude	Longitude	Speed	RPM	Speed	Dir		Dir	Ft	

_____

Signed

NAUTICAL LOG

Date

From: _____   Towards: _____

Time	Course	Log	Comments	Watch Leader
0100				
0200				
0300				
0400				
0500				
0600				
0700				
0800				
0900				
1000				
1100				
1200				
1300				
1400				
1500				
1600				
1700				
1800				
1900				
2000				
2100				
2200				
2300				
2400				

Watches Set

Time	Leader	Crew	Time	Leader	Crew

NAUTICAL LOG

Constant Port: _____ 1st High Water: _____ 1st Low Water: _____

_____ 2nd High Water: _____ 2nd Low Water: _____

Local Port: _____ 1st High Water: _____ 1st Low Water: _____

_____ 2nd High Water: _____ 2nd Low Water: _____

M Compass			Position		Boat		Wind		Barometer	Sea State		Sky Cond
Varia	Devia	True	Latitude	Longitude	Speed	RPM	Speed	Dir		Dir	Ft	

_____

Signed

NAUTICAL LOG

Date

From: _____   Towards: _____

Time	Course	Log	Comments	Watch Leader
0100				
0200				
0300				
0400				
0500				
0600				
0700				
0800				
0900				
1000				
1100				
1200				
1300				
1400				
1500				
1600				
1700				
1800				
1900				
2000				
2100				
2200				
2300				
2400				

Watches Set

Time	Leader	Crew	Time	Leader	Crew

NAUTICAL LOG

Constant Port: _____   1st High Water: _____   1st Low Water: _____

_____   2nd High Water: _____   2nd Low Water: _____

Local Port: _____   1st High Water: _____   1st Low Water: _____

_____   2nd High Water: _____   2nd Low Water: _____

M Compass			Position		Boat		Wind		Barometer	Sea State		Sky Cond
Varia	Devia	True	Latitude	Longitude	Speed	RPM	Speed	Dir		Dir	Ft	

_____
Signed

NAUTICAL LOG

Date

From: _____   Towards: _____

Time	Course	Log	Comments	Watch Leader
0100				
0200				
0300				
0400				
0500				
0600				
0700				
0800				
0900				
1000				
1100				
1200				
1300				
1400				
1500				
1600				
1700				
1800				
1900				
2000				
2100				
2200				
2300				
2400				

Watches Set

Time	Leader	Crew	Time	Leader	Crew

NAUTICAL LOG

Constant Port: _____   1st High Water: _____   1st Low Water: _____

_____   2nd High Water: _____   2nd Low Water: _____

Local Port: _____   1st High Water: _____   1st Low Water: _____

_____   2nd High Water: _____   2nd Low Water: _____

M Compass			Position		Boat		Wind		Barometer	Sea State		Sky Cond
Varia	Devia	True	Latitude	Longitude	Speed	RPM	Speed	Dir		Dir	Ft	

_____

Signed

NAUTICAL LOG

Date

From: _____ Towards: _____

Time	Course	Log	Comments	Watch Leader
0100				
0200				
0300				
0400				
0500				
0600				
0700				
0800				
0900				
1000				
1100				
1200				
1300				
1400				
1500				
1600				
1700				
1800				
1900				
2000				
2100				
2200				
2300				
2400				

Watches Set

Time	Leader	Crew	Time	Leader	Crew

NAUTICAL LOG

Constant Port: _____ 1st High Water: _____ 1st Low Water: _____

_____ 2nd High Water: _____ 2nd Low Water: _____

Local Port: _____ 1st High Water: _____ 1st Low Water: _____

_____ 2nd High Water: _____ 2nd Low Water: _____

M Compass			Position		Boat		Wind		Barometer	Sea State		Sky Cond
Varia	Devia	True	Latitude	Longitude	Speed	RPM	Speed	Dir		Dir	Ft	

_____
Signed

NAUTICAL LOG

Date

From: _____   Towards: _____

Time	Course	Log	Comments	Watch Leader
0100				
0200				
0300				
0400				
0500				
0600				
0700				
0800				
0900				
1000				
1100				
1200				
1300				
1400				
1500				
1600				
1700				
1800				
1900				
2000				
2100				
2200				
2300				
2400				

Watches Set

Time	Leader	Crew	Time	Leader	Crew

NAUTICAL LOG

Constant Port: _____   1st High Water: _____   1st Low Water: _____

_____   2nd High Water: _____   2nd Low Water: _____

Local Port: _____   1st High Water: _____   1st Low Water: _____

_____   2nd High Water: _____   2nd Low Water: _____

M Compass			Position		Boat		Wind		Barometer	Sea State		Sky Cond
Varia	Devia	True	Latitude	Longitude	Speed	RPM	Speed	Dir		Dir	Ft	

_____
Signed

NAUTICAL LOG

Date

From: _____   Towards: _____

Time	Course	Log	Comments	Watch Leader
0100				
0200				
0300				
0400				
0500				
0600				
0700				
0800				
0900				
1000				
1100				
1200				
1300				
1400				
1500				
1600				
1700				
1800				
1900				
2000				
2100				
2200				
2300				
2400				

Watches Set

Time	Leader	Crew	Time	Leader	Crew

NAUTICAL LOG

Constant Port: _____   1st High Water: _____   1st Low Water: _____

_____   2nd High Water: _____   2nd Low Water: _____

Local Port: _____   1st High Water: _____   1st Low Water: _____

_____   2nd High Water: _____   2nd Low Water: _____

M Compass			Position		Boat		Wind		Barometer	Sea State		Sky Cond
Varia	Devia	True	Latitude	Longitude	Speed	RPM	Speed	Dir		Dir	Ft	

_____
Signed

NAUTICAL LOG

Date

From: _____   Towards: _____

Time	Course	Log	Comments	Watch Leader
0100				
0200				
0300				
0400				
0500				
0600				
0700				
0800				
0900				
1000				
1100				
1200				
1300				
1400				
1500				
1600				
1700				
1800				
1900				
2000				
2100				
2200				
2300				
2400				

Watches Set

Time	Leader	Crew	Time	Leader	Crew

NAUTICAL LOG

Constant Port: _____ 1st High Water: _____ 1st Low Water: _____

_____ 2nd High Water: _____ 2nd Low Water: _____

Local Port: _____ 1st High Water: _____ 1st Low Water: _____

_____ 2nd High Water: _____ 2nd Low Water: _____

M Compass			Position		Boat		Wind		Barometer	Sea State		Sky Cond
Varia	Devia	True	Latitude	Longitude	Speed	RPM	Speed	Dir		Dir	Ft	

_____
Signed

www.ingramcontent.com/pod-product-compliance
Lightning Source LLC
Chambersburg PA
CBHW080658190526
45169CB00006B/2177